Unreasonable Brutality

By James M. Thayer

For my Lord,

I may never have the right words to honor
You with, but I will still try because You are
exceedingly worthy.

Seek First Productions, LLC – established 2012

Text copyright © 2023 James M. Thayer
All rights reserved.

ISBN: 979-8-9877867-3-4

Library of Congress Control Number: 2023908953

Contents

Introduction

In each of the gospels (the four books of the bible that record the life, death, and resurrection of Jesus), readers must endure the story of Jesus' crucifixion. As someone who has read the gospels dozens of times, this portion of the story has historically made me wince. I'm often tempted to skip it because it is the climax of everything wrong in our world. Seemingly, evil triumphs over good, foolishness defeats wisdom, justice gives way to corruption, etc. Everything about the story makes one's heart scream, "This isn't fair!" Yet, as followers of the Man of Sorrows, we know that the moment Satan thought he had triumphed, he was undone. JRR Tolkien, the author of the Lord of the Rings series, called this moment (when paired with the Resurrection of Jesus) a eucatastrophe. That is, a *good* catastrophe. When everything looked bleakest for the Kingdom of God, victory came.

It is this bleakness I desire to write about because it wasn't until a couple of years ago I started to read the gospels through a new lens. God interrupted my

"Christianity on life support" and opened my eyes to the Holy Spirit's work in the lives of believers. I began to ask the Holy Spirit to teach me God's word, and suddenly, everywhere I looked, I saw *things* moving behind the scenes in scripture. For twenty years, I ignored what precisely the Spirit of God was doing throughout the bible, and as such, I always missed what Satan was doing, too. Now, with different vision, the passion of Jesus (passion, meaning *suffering*) hit me even harder. I not only thought about how all the men in scripture mistreated our Lord as He was led to Golgotha, but I now thought about why, exactly, they mistreated Him so fiercely. The mocking He received, and the brutality He endured, was not reasonable - not even considering one of the most charitable reasons to use torture (to warn others not to commit crimes).

Imagine, for a moment, you are part of the religious mob that came to arrest Jesus in the middle of the night. You see Judas, your paid informant, kiss the one whose ministry you envy. As the servant of the high priest approaches, one of Jesus' students pulls his sword out of its sheath. He then tries to cut the servant's head off, but barely misses, and manages to cleave an ear. The servant is now screaming in agony; the temple police you're with all bring their swords out too. A battle is about to ensue. You then see Jesus, the "heretic", reprove His student and demand he sheathe his sword. People calm down, and somehow peace presses into your heart. The one known to you as a "blasphemer" now approaches the distraught servant and touches the side of his face where blood profusely pours from. Jesus removes His hand, and there you see it. The impossible. A new ear on the side of the servant's head. The mob you are part of arrests Jesus, despite this, and not very long after, you'll demand His crucifixion.

As believers, we read this passage and have the rational audacity to protest, "Really? You're going to put *that* guy to death? You *just* saw a miracle – an amputee received his appendage back! Yet, Jesus is the one you're going to mock and beat and turn over to the Romans to be brutalized and crucified?"

One would think, upon seeing such a miracle, the mob would have re-thought its plan. Remember, it wasn't just this one miracle they saw that night. John's gospel records that as the arresting party approached, Jesus asked them who they were looking for. When they answered, "Jesus of Nazareth," Jesus responded, "I am He," and the mob literally fell backward onto the ground. Seriously, *that's* the guy you're going to put to death? It makes no sense from a purely rational perspective.

In Matthew 26, verse 68, we're told the religious leaders of the Sanhedrin (a Jewish court) beat Jesus and then demanded, "Prophecy to us, Messiah, who hit you!" In Isaiah 50:6 we read, "I offered my back to those who beat me, my cheeks to those who pulled out my beard; I did not hide my face from mocking and spitting." They pulled Jesus' beard out; they spit on Him; they not only savagely beat Him but dared to then mock His claim to be the Messiah. There was a simultaneous *denial of His power* and a *mocking of the things of God*. This was done by the hands of the Jewish leaders of Jesus' day - the most respected, and those supposedly living closest to God. How then, could they both mock God to His face so brazenly and deny His power?

Whether we look at the religious leadership, the Roman politic, or even Jesus' own followers, we find unreasonable actions, passions, and brutality. The passion of Jesus is dripping with beyond-the-pale evil. Why would Pilate, after deciding Jesus was innocent, turn Him over for death anyway? Why would the people welcoming Jesus into their town with palm leaves and praises of "Hosanna," not but five days later demand Him to be crucified? Why would a Roman citizenry vote to have Barabbas, a violent man, freed over the Prince of Peace? Why was so much energy spent mocking Jesus? Why did He receive such a brutal beating and death despite no crime? A crown of thorns was shoved on His head to mock His claim to be a King and deny His power, even though they saw that same power for years!

Usually, when a government decides to execute a person, it does so dispassionately. The execution of Jesus, though, had all the hallmarks of a man being slaughtered for stealing someone's wife or killing their small children. It is possibly one of the most cared-for executions in history. There was such great *revelry* from the actors. People *delighted* to see Jesus tortured and murdered. Though one later repented, even the crucified thieves somehow found the strength to mock Jesus with their final breaths. From a purely human perspective, the whole thing is an outrageous scene.

But to look at it through merely human eyes is to make a mistake. It is like seeing the top of an iceberg and failing to account for its foundation beneath the waves. Behind the spitting, the jeers, the beating, the yelling, the whipping, nailing, contempt, and fear - was a demonic realm at feast. In Luke 22:3, we are told the exact moment Satan entered Judas. Here's a man that walked with Jesus, healed the sick, drove out demons, and collected baskets full of leftovers from the miraculous feeding of multitudes. He saw Jesus walk on water and saw dead people brought back to life. Yet, we are told he loved money, and through that love of money, Satan came and had his way with Judas. If a man like him could become a pawn of Satan, how about the Pharisees and Sadducees, the scribes and Roman soldiers – and what about *us*?

This story has a warning for all of us, but there is also great hope. We know, scripturally, the brutality Jesus endured likewise procured our healing (Isaiah 53:5). His pain resulted in the amelioration of our own. In the following few brief chapters, I want to explore both this warning, and this hope.

Scourge

"...His appearance was so disfigured beyond that of any human being and his form marred beyond human likeness." – Isaiah 52:14

No one living today has seen a flogging like the ones meted out by Roman lictors at the whipping post. Of course, there are documented cases of modern-day canings and whippings, but no matter how severe, they do not measure up to the ones criminals endured under Rome. Nevertheless, we have several modern harrowing eyewitness accounts that can illuminate us. One such description comes from Two Years Before the Mast, written by Richard Henry Dana in 1839. In it, Dana tells a story about a man named Sam who fights with the captain of their freighter traveling the Pacific Ocean. The man is bested, tied up, and flogged with a "cat o nine tails" – a whip with nine cords that contain up to three knots each. After the first strike, the man is silent; upon the second, he mutters in pain, and as the strikes continue, the man is undone. Eventually, Sam is cut down and let go.

Another man on the ship, named John, asks the captain why Sam was flogged, which enrages the captain and lands John in hot water. Dana wrote what happened next:

"When [John] was made fast [tied up], he turned to the captain, who stood turning up his sleeves and getting ready for the blow, and asked him what he was to be flogged for. 'Have I ever refused my duty, sir? Have you ever known me to hang back, or to be insolent, or not to know my work?'

'No," said the captain, 'it is not that I flog you for; I flog you for your interference - for asking questions.'

'Can't a man ask a question here without being flogged?'

'No,' shouted the captain; 'nobody shall open his mouth aboard this vessel, but myself'; and began laying the blows upon his back, Swinging half round before each blow, to give it full effect. As he went on, his passion increased and he danced about the deck calling out as he swung the rope: 'If you want to know what I flog you for, I'll tell you. It's because I like to do it! - because I like to do it! It suits me! That's what I do it for!'

The man writhed under the pain, until he could endure it no longer, when he called out, with an exclamation more common among foreigners than with us - 'Oh, Jesus Christ, oh, Jesus Christ!'

'Don't call on Jesus Christ,' shouted the captain. 'He can't help you. Call on Captain T - He's the man! He can help you! Jesus Christ can't help you now!'

At these words, which I never shall forget, my blood ran cold. I could look on no longer. Disgusted, sick, and horror-struck, I turned away and leaned over the rail, and looked down into the water. A few rapid thoughts of my own situation, and of the prospect of future revenge, crossed my mind; but the falling of the blows and the cries of the man called me back at once.

At length they ceased, and turning round, I found that the mate, at a signal from the captain, had cut him down. Almost doubled up with pain, the man walked forward and went down into the forecastle. Everyone else stood still at his post, while the captain, swelling with rage and with the importance of his achievement, walked the quarter-deck." – Two Years Before the Mast

Although this flogging was nowhere near as brutal as a Roman one before crucifixion, it is still challenging to read as it offends our sense of morality. At first, we're told John is beaten for asking a simple question, but later we find out his tormentor is whipping him simply because he enjoys doing it. The captain revels in administering torture. Why is that?

CS Lewis once wrote about two things inside him that were competing with the human self he desired to be:

"The sins of the flesh are bad, but they are the least bad of all sins. All the worst pleasures are purely spiritual: the pleasure of putting other people in the wrong, of bossing and patronizing and spoiling sport, and back-biting; the pleasures of power, of hatred. For there are two things inside me, competing with the human self which I must try to become. They are the Animal self, and the Diabolical self. The Diabolical self is the worse of the two. That is why a cold, self-righteous prig who goes regularly to church may be far nearer to hell than a prostitute. But, of course, it is better to be neither."

He claims there is an animal self, with all its base desires like misusing sex or alcohol, which we can sum up as hedonism and instinct. But there is also the diabolical self which isn't content with merely following one's instinct, but it must destroy the instinct – supersede it and replace it with something sinister.

Let me borrow an example from the animal kingdom for a moment. When a lion eviscerates a gazelle, he is most interested in the animal being quickly apprehended, killed, and put in his stomach. Why? Because the lion is hungry. He has an instinct to eat and knows he needs nutrients to live. He doesn't try to make the death of the gazelle more painful than it needs to be, nor does he take particular care to make it less painful than it needs to be; his focus isn't really on anything other than filling his belly.

In contrast, the prior-mentioned captain doesn't have a base instinct to be filled by whipping a man. If anything, beating John within an inch of his life is irrational from an economic perspective – if John can't work effectively, then the ship won't be as profitable as it could be. The captain is doing it because it pleases him beyond his animal self. Without a doubt, I guarantee you, the captain is *demonized.* It shouldn't go without noticing that the captain simultaneously mocks Jesus and denies Jesus' power to save, as John cries for His help. This is typical of a *religious* spirit, but more on that later.

Other modern examples of flogging include the case described in Fifteen Lashes, written by Anwar Iqbal in 1980s Pakistan. Iqbal once attended a public flogging where multiple convicts (their crimes ranged from extra-marital affairs to drinking alcohol) were whipped in front of large crowds who were there to enjoy it, much like a football game. This is an excerpt from his eyewitness account:

"Two constables brought the convict on to the stage. He looked utterly helpless. He was not trembling. He did not even look afraid. He looked more like an animal about to be slaughtered and unable to understand what was happening to him. He could not follow verbal commands...There seemed to be no coordination between his thoughts and his actions. Each of his hands and feet appeared to be moving separately. The constables led him to the frame. Then the doctor came, examined him, listened to his heart with a stethoscope, and declared him fit for flogging. The man listened to the pronouncement with indifference, as if it did not concern him. He even nodded his head twice, as if endorsing the doctor's decision.

By now the crowd was completely silent. Even the hawkers, selling ice cream and fresh fruits to the crowd, were quiet. The constables lifted the man up on to the frame, and tied his hands and feet to the scaffolding: his face was turned towards the stage and his buttocks exposed to the crowd. They tied another piece of cloth above his hips to mark the target. Then they moved aside. Now all eyes were fixed on the whip-man who was fiercely slashing the air with his whip. The crowd was so quiet that the microphone picked up the slashing of the whip and carried it everywhere. The man on the scaffolding also heard the sound. So far he had been very quiet but the slashing sound changed him. He started trembling and then cried, very loudly. The loudspeakers carried his voice to the crowd and beyond, but nobody spoke a word.

Now a magistrate, also sitting on the stage, asked the

whip-man to begin. He tested the whip for the last time, slowly hitting his left palm, and then came running, stopped a foot or two from the scaffolding and hit the victim with full force. The whip touched his skin, went into his flesh and came out again. The man shrieked in agony. Those sitting on the stage could see blood oozing from the wound. "One," said the official counting the whips. The man was sobbing now which could be heard on the loudspeakers.

The whipper went back to his mark and came running again when the magistrate signaled him to resume. The whip hit the flesh, the man shouted for help, the flogger withdrew, came back again, hit him and withdrew. Once, this sequence was broken when the doctor came to examine the victim. After his examination, he invited the whip-man to continue. The constable untied the man after the fifteenth lash and he fell on to the stage. They removed him on a stretcher and brought the next man."

Iqbal, at first, was documenting the floggings to write against their use, but he would later write:

"Several months later I went to a maidan, a public space, in Rawalpindi where a blind woman was to be flogged for sexual misbehavior. An audience of hundreds of men

14

surrounded the stage where she was to be whipped. They displayed neither sorrow nor passion. They chatted about politics and sport as they waited for the flogging to begin.

Then a police officer came and asked them to go home because a higher court had suspended the flogging. Soon the maidan rang with voices of disapproval. The men wanted to watch the tamasha, the hullabaloo. They were there to watch the woman's helplessness and to enjoy it....And the truth was that I shared their disappointment. Although I had been writing against public flogging ever since it began, I wanted to watch it. I might go back to my typewriter and condemn it, but I did not want to miss the spectacle.

This was an unpleasant discovery to make about myself. A sorrowful, angry disgust -- with myself and the country I lived in -- thus became a feature of my life."

There are two things about this incident I want to touch on. The first is how such brutality became entertainment. One section of Iqbal's account I left out dealt with young adults who attended the flogging and who were guilty of the same crimes, namely, debauchery and sexual intercourse outside of marriage. The author states plainly that these people understood they were untouchable by the same laws because of their great wealth. In essence, they were buying drinks and munching on snacks - watching men who had committed the same crimes they had, be tortured. And they enjoyed it.

I've already mentioned how the religious spirit mocks the things of God while denying His power, but parallel to these traits is hypocrisy rooted in self-righteousness. Jesus warned the religious leaders of His day that they were like white-washed tombs. They looked clean on the outside, but only dead men's bones were on the inside. He also likened them to people who only clean the outside of a cup while leaving the inside filthy (Matthew 23). Such people may look pious to those around them, but God sees their heart and knows it is profoundly sinful.

The problem for religious people like this is the fact they, too, know they are profoundly sinful. But they must keep up appearances out of their stubborn pride. Their reputation means more to them than their reality. I've known drug addicts who pride themselves on not being addicted to substances they believe are only reserved for *real* addicts. I've seen white-collar criminals who steal from their clients and vendors look down upon looters who steal from small businesses. This type of person is the one whom Jesus said fails to see the plank in their own eye while they attempt to remove a speck of dirt from their brother's eye (Matthew 7).

When they see people caught in a particular brand of sin they think they are above, it doesn't make them question their own heart. In fact, it does the opposite. Instead, they use the other person to say, "Well, at least I'm not *that* bad." Similarly, Jesus once gave a parable about a tax collector and a Pharisee. A Pharisee in the New Testament bible was a member of a particular sect of Judaism, which was quite strict in its religious duties. These were considered the holiest of men in their time, and yet they took the brunt of Jesus' scorn for their self-righteousness, hypocrisy, and general blindness to-ward the things of God.

In this parable, a tax collector (who most likely was extorting people) stands at a distance in the temple to pray to God. He recognizes that he is a sinner, and then asks God to have mercy on him. A Pharisee also prays to God. However, his prayers are very different. Instead of recognizing his own sin, he chooses to see it in the tax collector. He thanks God that he isn't like the tax collector or other "evildoers" and gloats about his righteous deeds. Jesus concludes by stating the tax collector, and not the Pharisee, went home justified before God (Luke 18).

Notice the Pharisee took great pleasure in looking down upon the tax collector. Instead of loving the sinner, desiring his good, and considering the tax collector more important than himself, he condemned him in his heart. I venture to say this Pharisee would have liked nothing more than to see the tax collector scourged for his crimes. I can hypothesize this based on two other biblical scenarios – the first is that religious leaders wanted to punish Jesus for even doing good things, like healing people on the Sabbath (Matthew 12). The second scenario is the stoning of the woman caught in adultery (John

7). But remember, as soon as Jesus told them they could start throwing stones if they had not sinned, people began walking away. The Bible records the oldest left first – perhaps because they were wiser, or maybe because they had collected more sin by that time. Either way, introspection made them understand a simple fact: they all deserved to be stoned.

That crowd came with zeal but left dejected, and rightfully so. A pastor once told me that it would be horrifying if we all had a TV screen above our heads that broadcasted our every thought. Imagine the young men attending the flogging of other young men for crimes they, too, had committed. Do you think there would be delight or terror in their hearts if their sins were broadcast this way? The problem is, even with their sins broadcasted, the religious spirit inside them may be more upset that their reputation was ruined than truly grieved that they had sinned against God and needed to repent (2 Corinthians 7:10). Most likely, they would be predominately interested in what everyone else's TVs were broadcasting and say, "Well, at least I didn't do that!"

I must imagine everyone involved in the execution of Jesus was convicted of their sins in one form or another, at least by the end. Pilate's wife warned him that she had a dream about Jesus, and that Jesus was a righteous man. Pilate knew Jesus was innocent and washed his hands of the crime about to unfold, but had Him scourged anyway. Later, Pilate would nail a sign next to Jesus, calling Him the "King of the Jews," for that is who he believed Jesus to be. But he crucified Him still. Why?

Well, let's examine another aspect of Iqbal's account. He wrote that there was a time he went to attend the flogging of a blind woman, and the event was canceled. He said it shocked him *that* he was disappointed. For in himself, he found what C.S. Lewis warned us about – the diabolical self. Something he considered sorrowful and disgusting pleased him, becoming a feature of his life.

Have you known someone who has experienced, or experienced yourself, the slippery slope of sin? People who set out to habitually sin believe they have control over it – that's part of its initial allure. They might start out saying, "I'll just look at some pornography now and again, but I won't make it a feature of my life," and ten years later, they find it has become an uncontrollable urge – one they are disgusted by, but likewise one they can't quit. Maybe they started out looking at relatively tame images. Still, it wasn't enough for them after some time, so they delved deeper into darker forms of it until they found their natural sexual function was no longer natural, but something else entirely.

Or perhaps you've known someone who had similar experiences with fear – requiring more vivid and darker experiences to get the same high out of being scared as they started with. Or maybe it was drugs that turned into a severe dependency, or control which turned into OCD, or entertainment which turned into an inability to focus or overcome boredom on one's own, or contrarianism that turned them into a bitter shell of a human. A million pathways describe the same condition – something a person thought was harmless, or which they once may have even found disgusting, eventually turned into an enslaver they couldn't live without. For Pilate, it may have been his authority or reputation; it probably was *fear* of inciting a riot that led him to the irredeemable act of turning over an innocent Man to scourging and eventual death. For Judas, his greed took him so captive a literal demon was able to enter him, and he sold the Author of life itself for thirty silver pieces. For Peter, it was an ignorant zeal that he thought would carry him to defend his Lord to the death, that required that same Lord to tell him bluntly, "Get behind me, Satan (Matthew 16)." And when Peter's time of testing came, he melted like wax – denying Jesus three times. He became the very thing he maybe detested the most – a coward. Finally, Iqbal started as a man disgusted by the act of flogging and ended up one that delighted in the violence to the point of being disappointed when he couldn't see it afflicted on a blind woman.

We can see Satan moving on every page if we carefully read the gospels. This is a warning for us today – that while we eat, sleep, work, and play, we have a real enemy vying for space in our hearts and minds that should only be reserved for God.

My point in giving examples of *modern-day* floggings is to start opening our eyes a little to the sadistic nature of humans engaged in the practice today - so when I tell you it was *far* worse under Roman rule, you have footing to start on.

The Romans did not use a cane. Modern flogging in places like Indonesia often involves striking a person's back with a wooden cane - which leaves heavy bruising but doesn't typically break the skin. The "cat o nine tails," previously described, is closer to what was used on Jesus, but it is still very tame in comparison. No, the Romans used an instrument entirely in its own class to torture victims before their crucifixion. It was a device called a Flagrum. The Journal of American Medical Association describes it as such:

"The usual instrument was a short whip (flagrum or flagellum) with several single or braided leather thongs of variable lengths, in which small iron balls or sharp pieces of sheep bones were tied at intervals...As the Roman soldiers repeatedly struck the victim's back with full force, the iron balls would cause deep contusions, and the leather thongs and sheep bones would cut into the skin and subcutaneous tissues. Then, as the flogging continued, the lacerations would tear into the underlying skeletal muscles and produce quivering ribbons of bleeding flesh."

There wasn't just one man doing the scourging either. Instead, there would be a minimum of two lictors whipping. This helped keep them from getting tired too quickly and ensured the victim was scourged on both sides of his back. The whips would swing around to the man's front, sometimes resulting in losing an eye or ear.

When the *Jews* would flog someone, they were limited by the Law to 4o lashes, but when the *Romans* flogged someone, there was no such limit. Scourging would often lead to the death of its victim, but if that was the case, the lictors had done a poor job. Their job was to make the person suffer as much as possible without killing them, so they could still be crucified. Jesus would have been scourged in this

way, and as Isaiah wrote, He was so brutally muti-
lated that people couldn't stand to look at Him, nor
could they discern human likeness on Him.

An account states that when Mary, the mother of
Jesus, was brought to the three crucified victims to
see her son, she said, "Which one is He?" Even if
the account isn't accurate, the sentiment certainly
is.

Now, remember what we've discussed presently
about the diabolical self, regarding these floggings.
People genuinely learn to enjoy such spectacles.
Lictors were professional torturers commanded to
make victims feel as much pain as possible while
sparing their lives. If the captain in our first account
of flogging mentioned enjoyed the act, how much
more would these Romans? After all, it was their
life's work, a *feature* of their life.

Pair this understanding with what we know about
Satan. He delights in killing, in stealing, in destroy-
ing. Demons view humans as things to tempt to-
ward sin, bind, and bring to death through sickness
or suicide or murder, if possible. What do you think
they would do if they got their hands on the Son of

God and were allowed to have their way with Him?
You better believe no one was scourged as severely
as Jesus, nor had demons delighted and feasted as
well as they did prior to that day. We know Jesus'
scourging must have been exceedingly terrible because of how quickly He perished on the cross. Romans were used to their victims taking days to die
through crucifixion, but our Lord only lasted about
six hours before expiring. He had already given so
much of His flesh and blood before He even started
to mount Golgotha where He was crucified.

Remember, our Lord needed another man's help to
carry His cross. The beam is estimated to have
weighed 165 pounds and would have further evis-
cerated His shoulders as he carried it. He would
eventually be nailed to this beam– his back, now
unbelievably lacerated, exposed to the tree as He
tried lifting Himself to gather a breath before tiring
out. He would have had to repeat this process for
each breath – the wood digging into His wounds
each time.

People died during crucifixion from asphyxiation,
usually. They got too tired to lift themselves up to
take a breath and suffocated. That is why the Ro-

mans were about to break Jesus' legs at one point – because without legs, the victim could not gain any more breaths.

Friend, there aren't enough words to effectively describe the physical pain our Lord endured. I once received an impression from the Holy Spirit of just what Jesus went through during this time. God didn't actually let me see it in a vision, but the terribleness of it was pushed upon my mind, and it broke me completely. I kept asking God, "How, How, How?" over and over again like a skipping CD, as I sobbed. I was trying to ask Him, "How could you love people that much to endure such agony for them?" Finally, in His mercy, the Lord responded to my petition. He said simply, "You do not need to know how, just know it is true."

This entire conversation was housed in the fact God had revealed to me that I would pray for thousands of people in my lifetime, and He would heal them. We know, from scripture, the only reason this is possible is because Jesus endured the scourging. As Peter wrote, "By His [Jesus'] wounds, you have been healed (1 Peter 2:24)." This one verse, which echoes what Isaiah wrote in Isaiah 53:5, has rightfully given hope to billions of believers throughout time.

Hope

"This was to fulfill what was spoken through the prophet Isaiah:

'He took up our infirmities

and bore our diseases.'" – Matthew 8:17

While our Savior endured unreasonable torture at the hands of lictors, Roman soldiers, and Jewish leaders – Satan was having a field day. He may have thought, in his pride, that he had finally won the war against God. Who knows how long his cosmic rebellion had gone on before this moment? Satan had rebelled and taken an angel army with him. He managed to tempt Adam and Eve – marring the image of God with the knowledge of good and evil. This effectively separated humanity from its Creator for thousands of years.

Our enemy knew God had set a counterattack in motion, and at every turn, Satan seemed to prevail.

Prophets would come, and Satan would have them put to death. Jesus was no different to him. He knew this was the Christ, the Son of God, and as Jesus breathed His last, Satan probably began to celebrate too early – the hallmark of hubris.

But with every torn piece of flesh, with each thorn plunging into His brow, with each nail piercing His body, Jesus was doing something magnificent. He did not resist any of this torture. Instead, He remained silent and endured. He could have called down legions of angel armies (Matthew 26) to save Him from this terrible fate. But our Lord did not. Why?

The answer is almost too awful to write.

Heaven went bankrupt, giving up its Crown Jewel, for *me*, for *you*, for anyone who would look upon that disfigured and broken body and put their faith in Him.

This singular obedience to His Father, the most significant showing of servitude humanity had ever seen, and a sacrifice beyond our comprehension – brought salvation to untold numbers of people. It wasn't just unreasonable brutality at the hands of men, goaded on by Satan, that Jesus endured. He likewise took the wrath of God on our behalf.

"But God demonstrates his own love for us in this: While we were still sinners, Christ died for us. Since we have now been justified by his blood, how much more shall we be saved from God's wrath through him!" – Romans 5:8-9

I possess neither the vocabulary nor revelation to fully describe what this meant for our Lord. He became a curse (Galatians 3:13); He became sin itself (2 Corinthians 5:21). John describes Jesus as the "propitiation" for our sins (1 John 4:10). A Propitiation is an act used to satisfy the wrath of God. Isaiah 53:10-11 reminds us:

"Yet it was the will of the Lord to crush him; he has put him to grief; when his soul makes an offering for guilt, he shall see his offspring; he shall prolong his days; the will of the Lord shall prosper in his hand. Out of the anguish of his soul he shall see and be satisfied; by his

knowledge shall the righteous one, my servant, make many to be accounted righteous, and he shall bear their iniquities."

The death of Jesus was the perfect marriage between justice and mercy. If God is perfectly just, then He can't forgo punishing evil. If God is perfectly merciful, then He can't fail to extend mercy to those condemned by their wickedness. From a human perspective, God put Himself into a real pickle when He determined to give us free will – knowing we would reject Him and sin and incur His wrath. He wanted children to live with Him forever in perfect union. How could He achieve that and not deny His own nature? The only solution was the cross.

The cross satisfied justice – for God's wrath was poured out for the sins of us all – which were placed upon Christ. The cross satisfied mercy – for anyone who puts their faith in Jesus for their atonement and makes Him their Lord will have their record of sin wiped clean. This is called the Great Exchange. Jesus received our iniquities, and we received His righteousness – for He lived the perfect life, having never sinned. So when God looks at His children, you and I, we are justified before Him. An easy way to remember what "justified" means is by saying, "just-as-if-I never sinned." God has not only forgiven your sin but has forgotten it (Hebrews 8:12). There is hope for those dead in their sin – His name is Jesus.

Many believers can get this far in their theology. They recognize they were once dead in their sins, God loved them, and He made a way by the blood of Jesus to be reconciled back to Him. But that is not the end of the story. Jesus not only nailed our sins to the cross, but He nailed our sickness and disease, our slavery to darkness, and our losses *due* to that darkness, also. Put succinctly, Jesus came to "sozo" us, which is a Greek word that translates into "save, heal, deliver, and restore."

I once prayed for a woman who had converted to Christianity and tried hard to overcome her old life. As she described everything she had fallen into – depression, promiscuity, fear, addiction, etc. – I be-

gan to see a picture in my mind. I saw a person
struggling because they had large meat hooks
lodged in their shoulders and back, which were at
the ends of thick metal chains that were ultimately
connected to a massive concrete block. The person
was struggling to move forward but could not break
free. I described this picture to the woman, who
agreed it was how she felt. Like Paul in Romans 7,
she said she wanted to do good things but could not
– that the things she did do she did not want to do.
In a word, she was "bound."

On another occasion, I was preaching in a movie
theater after a showing – inviting people for prayer.
One of the women in the audience came up to me
sobbing and shaking – she could barely speak
through her pain. She told me she had been living
with severe depression and anxiety for a long time
and recently had done prison ministry. At the prison, she told inmates they could have joy if they put
their faith in Jesus. She cried to me, "How can I tell
them they can have joy when I don't have any myself?" This woman, too, was bound.

Once, I had finished praying for a little girl in the hospital when I asked her mom if there was anyone else in the ICU I could pray for. She said the floor was pretty cleared out, but a grown man a few rooms over had come in the night before, fighting, cursing, and screaming. I told the woman I must pray for the man, so she pointed me to his room. I poked my head in and asked, "Does anyone here need prayer?"

A middle-aged couple, obviously the parents, and a roughly 17-year-old man, were sitting in the middle of the room. The young man looked me dead in the eyes and said, "I need prayer." He explained what he had done to wind up at the hospital. He fought with his parents, drank an entire bottle of liquor, hopped in his car, and drove down the interstate as fast as he could. Since this was the fourth time he had done this, he was being sent to an institution after his hospital stay. I told him, "People do drugs or abuse alcohol because they are coping with something. What are you coping with?" He replied, "I have OCD, depression, anxiety, and I'm bipolar." Like the two women I've mentioned, this man was also bound by our enemy.

When we isolate only one fruit of Jesus' sacrifice –
the salvation it brought – we do not preach the
whole gospel (the word "gospel" means "good
news"). Instead, we only give people hope for the
life to come, and as such, they start to believe false
doctrines and live under condemnation from our
enemy. He'll tell them things like, "If you were just
more disciplined, if you just read your bible more,
you wouldn't be dealing with this." Satan loves religion. He adores the concept that people must work
for their salvation, freedom, healing, and restora-
tion. All those self-help books you see in the isles of
shopping centers are the fruit of this philosophy –
the notion that somehow a broken thing can fix itself.

**"Are you so foolish? Having begun by the Spirit, are you
now being perfected by the flesh?" – Galatians 3:3**

Now, don't mistake what I'm saying here. I am not
condemning discipline, hard work, and self-
reflection. I'm saying there comes a point where all

those things fall short. If you've ever known a suicidal person, you know exactly what I'm talking about. They can't do the things they need to do to get better because darkness has clouded their thoughts too much. Advice to eat right, exercise, and get out of the house sounds absurd to the person who no longer wants to even breathe. There is nothing outside themselves they see that is worth living for. In fact, they've convinced themselves that all those other things (and people) would be better off if they were no longer around. They are bound by Satan. There is an evil spirit that holds them captive.

There is hope, though! Jesus came to deliver us in addition to saving us.

"The Spirit of the Lord is on me, because he has anointed me to proclaim good news to the poor. He has sent me to proclaim freedom for the prisoners and recovery of sight for the blind, to set the oppressed free, to proclaim the year of the Lord's favor." – Luke 4:18-19

The prisoners Jesus speaks about in this passage

aren't people physically in jail somewhere (although I don't blame people for wanting to interpret it that way). They are people who have been held captive by our enemy – bound by sin, fear, sickness, depression, and death. Jesus was led bound Himself, from the Garden of Gethsemane to the Jewish council, from there to multiple governors, to the whipping post, and soldiers' quarters. Jesus wasn't running. In fact, He told Peter to stand down after Peter struck the servant's ear off. Jesus went peacefully everywhere His tormentors desired – it was unreasonable to bind Him at all. Yet, He was bound so that we might be freed. In Him is freedom, and as John 8:36 declares, "So if the Son sets you free, you will be free indeed."

This freedom is a gift, not something that can be earned as religion might persuade you. Like salvation, freedom is a gift from God that comes through faith in Christ by the power of the Holy Spirit. It is available to all, freely given so no one may boast, and no one may charge for it. If you're wondering what happened to each of the people I mentioned earlier that our enemy bound – Jesus freed them.

Through simple prayer and faith that Jesus would do what He said He would do – demons were driven out of all three of these people, and the Holy Spirit flooded into the void left over, bringing peace, joy, and power. There is hope for the captive – His name is Jesus.

But Jesus didn't only come to save and deliver. He also came to heal us. I'm not talking about meta-phorical healing, but actual physical healing in our bodies. Scripture is clear that the scourging Jesus endured resulted in our recovery, and that our sick-ness and disease were placed upon Him at the cross. I'm not writing this book to give you a practical guide to pray for the sick but to honor my Lord by explaining just what it cost for us to be healed. His agony produced our joy, the anxiety He felt in the Garden brought us peace, the shedding of His blood was our salvation, and the breaking of His body – our healing. His reward is us – children brought near to God – saved, healed, delivered, and restored. So when churches do not pray for the sick to be healed, I believe they rob Christ of part of His re-ward. The Holy Spirit longs to apply healing procured at the cross. If only we would become vessels filled with Him and pray for the sick.

In 1990 a pastor named Duane Miller contracted a flu virus that penetrated the tissue of his vocal cords and permanently damaged the nerves beyond repair. Since his vocation required him to preach, Miller sought out 63 specialists, over the course of the following 2-3 years, to find treatment. Unfortunately, none could be found, and he was left with a screechy raspy voice that could only be heard if he screamed at the top of his lungs. With zero chance of recovery, Miller had to leave the pastoralship and then fumbled through multiple jobs – some of which did not pan out due to his communication problems.

He racked up thousands of dollars in medical bills while his wife became the primary provider for his family. He suffered mental anguish not being able to do the thing he most loved - preach. Then, one day, his bible study class asked him to fill in for the regular speaker and to give a lesson on Psalm 103. Despite a desire to preach again, Miller turned them down, saying they would not be able to hear him. The class knew he was depressed for this very reason, though, and prevailed upon him – even providing a special microphone to amplify his voice.

I have listened to a portion of his sermon from that day. One thing that stands out to me is Miller's theological take on Isaiah 53. He outright declares that the healing mentioned in scripture there is not physical. I, of course, protest this theology with every fiber of my being. Despite this, Miller does concede that God still heals people as he reads Psalm 103:3, which states, "Praise the Lord my soul and forget not all His benefits. He forgives all my sins and heals all of my diseases." As he read this passage, Miller recalls thinking, "I still believe God heals, but why does He not heal me?" He continued to read about how God redeemed the psalmist's (the person who wrote the passage) "life from the pit." Miller then told the bible study class, "I have had, and you have had, in times past, *pit* experiences."

The moment Miller said the word "pit," he recalls pressure that had been in his throat for years immediately came loose – it was as if a person had stopped choking him. Miller then attempted to carry on with his sermon, and his voice began to change. Eventually, he was overcome by God and was rendered speechless because he had been instantly, and miraculously, healed. Later he would visit multiple doctors who told him not only were his vocal cords perfect, but there was no sign they were ever damaged.

Despite Miller not understanding it, his healing was procured 2000 years prior at the cross of Calvary. Jesus bore his sickness in His body, and as He probably had difficulty speaking due to extreme thirst and anguish while hanging on that tree, Miller's voice was restored to him. Peter is clear on where our healing comes from – the wounds of Jesus (1 Peter 2:24).

I have been blessed to witness dozens of miraculous healings in my life. I've seen a woman's miscarriage cease and a baby delivered months later. I have seen people healed of autoimmune diseases, the effects of concussions, misaligned vertebrae, torn rotator cuffs, busted knees, and cancer – all instantly, by the power of the Holy Spirit. I once saw a woman with muscular dystrophy run for the first time in her entire life after God healed her during a thirty-second prayer. There is hope for the sick – His name is Jesus.

Battle

The combined martial genius of Napoleon, Alexander, Caesar, Rommel, Patton, and Jackson wouldn't even come close to rivaling Satan's.

The Church has constantly underestimated its enemy since the apostolic age - giving into the simplest of snares such as fellowship rivalry and self-conceit.

Many of our great modern Christian leaders have had shocking moral failings, which you don't have to live very long to hear about, and which I won't list here.

Our enemy has been eating saints, both great and small, for thousands of years - and yet many in the modern church plug their ears and refuse to believe he even exists. They behave as if he has already been thrown in the Lake of Fire. They don't engage in spiritual warfare because they don't believe they have to, and thus have already fallen in battle. Doctrines are created to neuter the Holy Spirit, Who is

our only effective weapon against the works of our
enemy, and so he takes ground effortlessly.

Without spiritual eyes, Christians then turn toward
their fellow man to find an enemy, and politics become the battlefield. Meanwhile, our true enemy
uses that same field as a decoy - allowing troops to
land on the shores of an unknown beach far away
from the true mark, to be bogged down in a fight
against paper targets - making any victory at all
meaningless in eternal consequence.

Satan has the most effective army any enemy could
desire. It is almost completely camouflaged. Unseen
by human eyes unless the Holy Spirit pokes and
prods enough to bring it to the surface. Lurking beneath our conscience, almost undetectable, the effects of which we mis-diagnose constantly. The
KGB could not have asked for better agents of sub-
version than our true enemy employs.

Entirely twisted by an unfathomable number of
years, our enemy hates God - and thus hates humanity made in God's image. Once tasting the full-
ness of the Spirit, Satan cannot stand the notion
such wretched creatures as ourselves might hold

that Glory within our frail bodies - destined for an
eternity in fellowship with the Creator. What envy
he must possess. The exports of his kingdom are
rotten fruit such as malice, pride, depression, and
self-righteousness. As such, he is the most miserable
of creatures, and you know what they say - misery
loves company.

Thus, hell was created for Satan, and he desires
bedmates in us. If he can succeed in supplanting the
gospel message, he'll have brotherhood in damna-
tion.

But Jesus died on a cross, Satan's ultimate victory -
murdering the Son of the Living God. Yet it was
pyrrhic in nature, for he won the battle and lost the
war. From depths of agony sprung hope, from dis-
figuring torture came healing, and from the darkest
day came bursting glorious light - the salvation of
man.

One night, if you can stomach it, read all four gospel accounts of the passion of Jesus back-to-back. It
is only a handful of pages, so it won't take long. As
you're reading, keep your eyes open for every time
Christ is mocked – the amount will astound you.

Moreover, these people really go out of their way to mock Him. The Roman soldiers, for example, not only beat Jesus but procured a scarlet robe and a scepter for Him. They harvested thorns and twisted them into a crown – undoubtedly hurting themselves in the process. They do all these things to mock a Person who never did anything wrong to them and refused to fight back. The entire scene is a profoundly irrational waste of energy. Yet, our enemy must have enjoyed it tremendously.

That enemy still exists today. He is called our enemy because he has set himself up as our personal torturer - desiring our downfall in this life and, if possible, the next. He has not been thrown into the lake of fire yet, and Peter even warns us that the devil is like a roaring lion looking to devour us this very day (1 Peter 5:8). For those who may not believe in demons, you must at least know a third of Jesus' miracles were driving unclean spirits out of people. If He was doing that while on Earth, where do you think all the demons have gone since then? They are still here.

Have you ever had a day like this? Maybe you woke up feeling just fine, but traffic was worse than you

expected on the way to work, and anger crept in –
stealing your joy. Or perhaps you heard about a guy
that got a big promotion, and instead of congratu-
lating him, envy crept into your mind, and you
started to criticize him in your heart. Maybe it was
something more blatant than these examples. Maybe one day you had a thought, a very tiny one, that
there was a chance life was meaningless. You began
to agree with this thought and eventually discov-
ered you were depressed. Or, for a moment, pretend
you laid to bed at night, and this thought entered
your mind: "Maybe there is no heaven. Maybe after
we die, there is nothing." You entertained this philosophy long enough that palpable fear overcame
you, and you now live with anxiety.

I do not know what plan of attack Satan has un-
leashed upon you. He has many avenues to take,
ranging from the perversion of our base desires to
self-righteousness. But I do know that no matter
how he is coming at you, the result he wants for
your life is the same – death. Physical death, spiritual death, the death of your joy and peace – what-
ever kind of death he can muster.

I hesitate to write this, but I believe it needs to be

said because I've witnessed it so many times at this point in my life. I have seen people miraculously delivered from things like depression, panic attacks, disease, and broken joints – but I have also seen all of these pains and mental sicknesses manifest again in their lives months, sometimes days, later.

It has taken me a long time to collect enough anecdotal data to hypothesize a reason for this, and my conclusion is quite apparent (though unsettling). Many of these people are healed and then subsequently *don't believe it.* I refuse to say this accounts for all instances, but certainly some. I once saw a woman, who was prayed for by another man, healed of an autoimmune disease she had since childhood. She later told me that 90% of her symptoms instantly disappeared overnight. But five days later, everything came back. I told her this was not uncommon, that I had seen it many times before, and I asked her why she thought it happened. Her response was, "I must admit that even though I was healed, the whole time I kept asking, 'But will this last?'"

Her enemy was the one asking that question, although she did not recognize it was him. The mo-

ment the question crossed her mind, she should
have engaged in spiritual warfare, "You deceitful
spirit, leave me now. The blood of Jesus has bought
me." Then, she should have stood firm on God's
word – that He had not given her a spirit of fear.
The way to discern whether what you're hearing is
from God or not is to cross reference it with His
word. If it does not align with His word, it is not
from Him. That means it is either from yourself or
from your enemy. Either way, submit the thought
to Jesus.

People who are delivered from depression and anxiety must know that those spirits come racing back
for them – Jesus promised us that much (Matthew
12). The question is, when they return to their old
home and begin to knock, will they be rejected or
let back in? I myself, upon conversion to Christianity, was delivered from depression. Likewise, I have
had to deny that spirit entrance back into my life at
least twice since that time. One of those times was
relatively recent.

My wife had been going through a challenging time
– her grandmother was in the hospital, and at the
same time, an excellent friend of hers had over-

dosed. She was worried about both and doing her best to care for them while managing her everyday responsibilities as a mother and wife. Our marriage became strained over a week during this time. It was obvious our enemy was working on her, and because of that, he began to work on me too. I heard a voice, "She doesn't like you."

It was a convincing voice because what it was saying aligned with what I was feeling. By this time in my life, I knew better that this wasn't *God's* voice. I knew it was my enemy. So I battled. I fought tooth and nail. I told my wife exactly what I was dealing with because the Holy Spirit directed me to do so. I then spent hours praying as I went about my day. That spirit of heaviness would lift and then come racing back. It would rise again and then come running back harder. I stood firm on the promises of God, though. I knew I had been set free from depression long ago, and I knew this was not His will for me.

By that evening, the spirit finally gave up. I had asked the Holy Spirit to drive it from me so many times; I had quoted scripture out loud to stand on truth; I had even asked my Heavenly Father to send a legion of angels to fight and torment the demon. When it finally lifted for good, I was flooded with greater joy than I had had for a long time.

But pretend for a moment I did not recognize the voice of my enemy. Pretend I did not battle and stand on God's word. Where might I be today? I shudder to think about what that seed of bitterness could have sprouted into. This is why it is so important for believers to wage spiritual warfare. Paul explicitly told us, "For our struggle is not against flesh and blood, but against the rulers, against the authorities, against the powers of this dark world and against the spiritual forces of evil in the heavenly realms (Ephesians 6:12)."

My wife wasn't my enemy; Satan was. Similarly – Pilate, the Jewish leadership, the soldiers, the lictors, etc., were not Jesus' true enemies. Yes, in one sense, all who are dead in sin are enemies of God, but my point is that Jesus loved those people. He was already interceding on their behalf when He asked God to forgive them – that they were ignorant (Luke 23:34). He could see straight through them, and He could see they were merely Satan's pawns doing his bidding. We must become aware of our true situation; it will change our lives. We're standing on a cosmic battlefield. If we keep our eyes closed to the Holy Spirit and our enemy, we will become those same pawns. This is the warning found in the passion story for all of us. This is the warning found in the story of the captain who flogged his sailor, John, merely because it suited him. This is the warning found in Iqbal's admission that he grew to enjoy watching the floggings in Pakistan: sin desires us. Satan desires us. They want to master us – to bend us to their will in advancing a kingdom of darkness on this Earth.

But Jesus brought hope. He went through excruciating (a word derived from "crucifixion") pain and terror. He endured unbearable, unthinkable, and unreasonable brutality so we might be saved, healed, delivered, and restored. So receive it, believe it, and when Satan comes to steal it from you – point him back to the cross where his power was undone. And always remember our Lord as you take communion. Remember the great sacrifice He made on our behalf. Remember that He considered it joy to endure what He did – because He was thinking of you.

"Therefore, since we are surrounded by such a great cloud of witnesses, let us throw off everything that hinders and the sin that so easily entangles. And let us run with perseverance the race marked out for us, fixing our eyes on Jesus, the pioneer and perfecter of faith. For the joy set before him he endured the cross, scorning its shame, and sat down at the right hand of the throne of God. Consider him who endured such opposition from sinners, so that you will not grow weary and lose heart."

– Hebrews 12:1-3